# My Life *in the* Service

## There is a God

HENRY ALKEMA

WestBow Press books may be ordered through booksellers or by contacting:

WestBow Press
A Division of Thomas Nelson & Zondervan
1663 Liberty Drive
Bloomington, IN 47403
www.westbowpress.com
844-714-3454

ISBN: 978-1-6642-4180-0 (sc)
ISBN: 978-1-6642-4181-7 (e)

Print information available on the last page.

WestBow Press rev. date: 9/21/2021

# My Life *in the* Service

# Prologue

---◆---

    Why did I write this book? There have been many times I have thought about it, but with the death of Gertrude, it became very clear that I should write my story for the enlightenment of my grandson. By the end, I hope he will see how the love of God through the Holy Spirit would make it possible for me to find a partner that would help me to walk my time on this earth with a purpose.

# Chapter 1

# There is a Holy Ghost? Ergo a God.

The early part of my life is very mundane, except at 9 months of life, I was adopted by a Dutch couple in Muskegon Michigan from adoption services in Detroit. At 5 years old, I was put in MacLaughlin Public School. About that time, my family built a new house close to the Dutch section of Muskegon and ergo, I went to the Dutch Christian School through the 10th grade. That was as far as it went – more grades came to the school in later years. In that school I had my mother's sister for English. If I got out of line my aunt would walk over to me and very softly say, "Bud, I don't want to talk to my sister." That took the fun out of that class.

After the tenth grade we transferred to Muskegon's public high school for grades eleven and twelve. I liked the school and had many friends. Graduating in February of 1946 from Muskegon High School, I went to work at Norge company to get the money to go on to a higher education. The company made refrigerators for the US on the first half of the week, and on the other half of the week, made fridges for Europe. The European fridges used metric measurement – way ahead of us. I was only there two months when I got pneumonia, went home and mom called the doctor because I was jumping up and down and screaming on my sister's bed on the downstairs, I could not breathe. Later, the doctor told me I had one third of one lung that was breathing. The other parts were full of liquid, so of no use. The doctor told my mother that there was no use of sending me to the hospital. It was too late. My mother walked over to the doctor and smacked him on his face, and he ran out of the house backward, saying "I will have everything ready." The doctor ran out of the house – yes, the doctors came to the houses in 1946. My family had a good friend with transportation and oxygen on board for going to the hospital.

The doctor was waiting for me in a room at the hospital with oxygen and a big plastic tent that covered my head and part of my chest. I remained under that cover and in a coma for 30 days. I was given a pill of sulfur every three hours, night and day, and a shot of penicillin every

4 hours. Before penicillin, the old way to cure was with sulfur and the chances were not good. The new way was with penicillin. It was put on the market because the war was over and no longer needed it for the soldiers and the war ended about 6 months before my pneumonia.

I did live, as you can tell, by reading this story. Once out of the hospital, I had to remain in my bed for one month. I read so much during this time that I had to get glasses. A little aside – my father just loved to tell the story of his wife smacking the doctor and the doctor running out of the house backward.

Following my "life" in bed, I worked driving a delivery truck. No more of the dirty work and also no more good money. In fall I went to school – Hope College – a Christian school and a good one.

Now we stop for a little background. If you know the Dutch reformed religion, you will know my religious upbringing. We worshipped the Trinity, God, Jesus, and Holy Spirit. But during my younger life, I had the feeling that being a not-so-bad-a person, the Holy Spirit had more work to do on the bad people and so would have little time for me. Very bad to have a value that limits God. Well, I was young, and about to learn much more. And now, with my wife gone to Heaven, I have been going back over how and why did God/Holy Spirit want me to have a wife from Europe? To help me grow up.

Dad, me, my brother, my sister, and my mom

# Joining the Air Force

Before the end of World War 2, I was called down to Detroit to be checked. I went down to Detroit and spent all day long urinating in bottles for medical tests and that kind of stuff. I was a 1A (I was available) and I was at that age where I was going to be picked in May or June of 1945. At the time, I was slated to go to school at Hope College in Holland, Michigan, having just finished high school. Would I be acceptable for service? Between the time of getting called and actually going to Detroit, the president said, "Bring all the troops home." So, all the Navy pitched war goods, ammunition, everything into the ocean to make room for troops. There was no consideration that these items might be needed a few years later, as generally, we have a war every 25 to 30 years.

Even though the war was officially over, they put me through the physical exams, and gave me an A1 stamp. After this, I was free to go to Hope College, but as I stated above, the Korean war started in 1950. I had been at Hope College for 2.5 years when in January 1950, I got a letter from the war office in Muskegon. There were 4 ladies there, and one of them went through her files and got mine from the exams in Detroit. My dossier had been sent from Detroit and sat there for five years. The woman said to me, "You're going to service in 10 days." I said, "No, I'm in school, so I don't have to go." She insisted, "No, you're leaving within 10 days." I said, "You're not listening to me," she said, "No, you're not listening to me. You are leaving in 10 days. Go home, and get things straightened out," and she was right.

My buddy at Hope was in the same boat. I said, "Well, we're not going to be forced into the Army, we already have one friend dead there. We're going to have to find a place in the Navy or the Air Force. Anything but the Army." There was a recruiting station in Muskegon to assign young men for the Korean war. My buddy and I went in. They were really looking for bodies now. The first recruiting office we came to was for the Air Force. We were told, as the man pointed to a large pile of files from people wishing to get into the Air Force, that, "I even have people from Kentucky." Again, the Holy Spirit as far as I'm concerned, was directing things. We asked him if we could take the test. My friend got 99%. I got 98%. He picked up the tests, said, "Watch," and put them right on top of the pile. He said, "We like people like you." In other words, we were smart enough. I said, "We've only got 5 days left, are you going to take care of this?" He said, "No problem, I've got it." We went home, got ready, and in 5 days, left for 8 weeks of Air Force training in San Antonio.

# Chapter 3

# Air Force Training

Being what I am, it was really "funny". What you are comes to the surface. There was a corporal that helped the sergeant with the new flight, which were 70 men. We were under his direction. The Corporal didn't like me, so he gave me the worst jobs. So, I said to the corporal, "Behind the latrine. You meet me at 7 o'clock and we're going to find out who's boss around here." He didn't show up, but the next morning I got a call from the office. Fortunately for me, the captain of our outfit was a very thoughtful and understanding person. All I was, was an airman with no stripes, no nothing. He said, "Airman, you invited the corporal to fight behind the latrine." I said, "Yes sir, he is picking on me, and I don't think he's smart enough to have that position anyhow." He smiled, and said to me, "You're in the Air Force now. Anyone who is above you, up to a General, can tell you what to do and you will say, "*Yes sir.* It doesn't have to be right and it doesn't have to be good. It's the way it is." I said, "But he's not too bright." He said, "You're not listening again. I know he's not too bright. He probably won't be high in the service but right now he's your boss. You do what he says, or I will send you home." In my mind I saw immediately that if I were to go home because I got kicked out dishonorably, then my father would be crushed. I could not besmirch my family name; it was not allowed. I think it goes back to a time when my father banged up my behind for doing something wrong in church. He told me, "Son, this is hurting me more than you son." Now, today I believe that because this was important to him, it was not my job to bring a bad name to our family. So, I shut up, and took the corporal's orders.

Later on, in training, we were practicing marching. For some reason, I did it right. I was able to manage turning and all of the steps. Seeing this, my sergeant chose me to be his right guard. In other words, when he was not present, I was to lead the boys around. He had the ability to growl at you, but also to talk to you as a real person. In his words, "If I am not present for whatever reason, you are in charge of the men." I was to drill them, take them to breakfast, etc. You see, he had the right to leave the base, and could be out on dates with the ladies in the evenings. Well, I did my job so well that at the end of the training, the captain called me in and said, "I'm proud of you. You did a real good job your sergeant has told me. Because of that, I'm going to make you Airman First Class." I got one stripe because of it and a little more money.

From the 8 weeks training, we were assigned to schools to continue studying. We were in a new flight with another 70 airmen. We were sent to the University of North Dakota to learn to be office administrators (or as the female sex would be called, a secretary—we also were called the "WAFs" which stood for "Women's Air Force." As I preferred to say at the time, we were the "titleless WAFs". Our job was basically to take attendance for the outfit, and to write letters for our superiors. If our boss wanted something from someone in the building, he'd send me out to get it.

# Chapter 4

# Headed to Europe

———❖———

We were there for a couple of months or so, and then we were sent to New Jersey. This was the camp from which those heading to Europe were dispatched. Those going to the Pacific were sent to San Francisco. I was one of the 6 heading to Europe to defend against the Soviets. Sixty-four of the group were heading for the war in Korea. You can be sure I was glad not to be going to Korea. I knew it was active war.

We weren't in New Jersey long- maybe a week or so- when we were assigned to boats and trucked or bused from the base to the boats and all I can say about the trip to Europe was that it was in August, and terribly hot. We would try to sleep on deck, but would be kicked off, only to try again later. They wanted us downstairs on our hammocks, but the bottom of a boat in August was barely livable. During the trip, my group was assigned to a building that had been the high office for the Luftwaffe Air Group.

Once in Germany, the boat let people off at various places, I was let off in Hamburg, Germany and from there took a train to Wiesbaden, a Rhein city 20 miles from Frankfurt.

The US Air Force got this building following the World War II and was still there during the Korean War. I was assigned to a major who was in charge of training for that building. In addition to the Major, I had an US Airman and a German national to help in the office. The only nice thing about that job was the days the major (who was a pilot in WWII) put in flying time (more money), going to places like Italy, Africa, Spain, etc. That day was well spent, and I got permission to fly the plane for about 5 minutes and then my Major said, "That is enough." He took the seat over and got the plane back on course. On this trip we went to Africa to deliver a small box of something. We had a lunch and one hour later we were on our way to Wiesbaden.

I did not like working for the Major or the job itself, so I was waiting for something to happen that would allow me to move on from this job.

It was springtime and someone up there decided the European Air Force should have a baseball team, wow! As I have played baseball before, I was going to try for the team. Got the paperwork from the top and left for Munich on the train. Things were going rather well on tryouts. I was trying for the position of a pitcher. But before about four weeks, the coach called 4 of us and said he had just received direction that he was to eliminate 4 more tryouts and I was one of them. So, I packed my belongings, waited for the bus to take us to Air Bases outside Munich where we had been reassigned. It was fun while it lasted.

I was assigned to an Air Force base outside of Munich where only planes of the US would land. Our specific duty was to repair the planes coming into our airport. We had Airmen that ran the tower and they would monitor in and outgoing planes so there would be no accidents. But, I was there only about six weeks when one of the Airmen upstairs on duty let out a big holler to the boys downstairs (I was one of them) to hurry upstairs because there was one of those new fighter planes that had wings that angled backward. He was coming to the base to have some work on it, that was what our base did.

By the time I got upstairs to the tower there was a fighter flying around the perimeter of the base trying to land but the wheels would not drop. Every time he came lower, he would shake the plane but they did not come down after he would try again. He had done this six times and told the boys in the tower he was running out of fuel and the next time around he had to come down and to tell his mother that he loved her.

The group on the base that tries to save a plane and or a pilot was done with its work. The runways were covered with six inches of some type of moist and slippery material so the plane could fly down the runway having no sparks and stop by the end of the runway. In addition, the medical people with their equipment were standing ready. He came floating in because of no fuel but he had it lined up perfectly. He was about 50 feet above landing and he started shaking the plane-I mean big time-it is going to crash anyway-so go for it. It wasn't more than 25 to 30 feet above the cement and the wheels began to drop and continue before landing. WOW! Everybody in our outfit started hollering, screaming, and hugging everybody there. God was there that day. I went downstairs to where the pilot checked in. I said, "That was a great job of flying." He just said, "Sometimes you win." That day is in my memory, like it was just yesterday.

There was a sergeant in the office who was in charge of me, a corporal. He had some good qualities: efficient, on time, neat and knew how to say, "Yes Sir." But all told, he was a bit goofy, his people skills were lacking ergo, he is not liked by the boys. He has never been in charge of a group of young men, and because he has a higher rank than most, he does not know how to use his power. We all get one month of time out each year and being in the middle of Europe the boys would travel to many places and countries. But not my boss, he took his one month to go home, Oklahoma- figure that out!

My officer boss was a man that was made for the job. He did his schooling at the army school, West Point, and then after WWII the president, Trumann, made the Air Force a separate group. Because the captain was in the Army Air Force, all he had to do was change his uniform to blue. He was not the type of officer to play soldier, but everyone in the outfit had to be very good at his job or they were gone.

My job was working in the office (a titleless WAF) we were called and how I hated it. It was mostly doing paperwork. About two or three months after joining the outfit, the captain called me into his office which was just across the aisle. He said, "The sergeant is going home for a month and do you think you can run the office, if you can, I will give you another strip." I thought no big deal but more money. I said, "Sir," this was the only officer in four years that I said sir to and meant it, "No problem, Sir, I do most of the work now and I can do it alone."

The month went quickly with no problems, so when the sergeant came back the captain called me into the office and handed me the paperwork with new name on it, Sergeant Henry J. Alkema and said, "I gave you the promotion and a good job." I said, "Thank you, sir, working for you was enjoyable."

A couple of months later, I thought that maybe I could discuss moving to a different job number. I thought that if I scratched your back you would scratch mine. So, about a month after I did my good duty and things were quiet and the captain wasn't doing anything extra important, I walked into his office. We had a little talk about me moving from my office job to the radio group. We talked about my dislike of the person I worked with as well as the job I was doing. I was not a happy camper. True to his colors, he said that I could give it a try and see how it will work out. Well, it worked very well as I drank beer with the radio boys, and I enjoyed that kind of work. Also, I checked in with the Captain and he was OK with the change.

# Chapter 5

# Austria

The road in back of Fox House.

I was doing fine in my job for about three to four months and enjoyed it, when I got called into the Captain's office. He said, "I got bad news here," and handed a letter from headquarters to me. I read it and just sat down. After a few minutes I asked the Captain if he could do anything to allow me to stay at this station as I was very happy with my new job. He said, "The order came from the headquarters and there is nothing I could do about that." I asked him when I had to leave, and he said, "ASAP." So, there goes another order and not on the way I wished to program my life.

The same "ole" story. Instead of a boat or airplane, I got a slow ride on a train from Munich to Vienna, Austria. From Vienna, I had a truck ride to my new station.

Wow! The buildings were beautiful. All the barracks were made of stone and the surroundings were hand made. This was a barracks made for Austrian soldiers. I never saw anything in the USA like this while I was in the Air Force. When I was assigned to a room, I would have it alone because it had only one bed for a single. It also had all of the necessities for "comfort" living. Also, it had a library, and most important, it had a bar with artisan German beer, guess what, 15 cents a bottle, big size for 16ml, about 20 ounce in English. Too bad I was in the service, as this could have been some easy living.

Now, on to the living. This Air Base was here because of the way the winners of WWII decided Austria would be divided into four sections, one for each winner: US, Russia, England and France. Vienna was in the middle of the Russian section, the city was divided the same way the country was, four parts, one for each of the four powers. When we went to Vienna, we had just one road to get there and it went to the US section of the city. If you went by train, which most of the boys did, because the train stopped beside the front gate and you were on it with a dozen steps. It ran close to the road and ended at St. Joseph train station which was in the US Section of the city.

A word about the Russians and the US in Austria. At the end of WWII at which time the four powers divided Austria up, rather than having a peace signing, they just hacked it up. Because our camp was in the Russian section, we had to move very carefully. When you were there the first thing you were told about where you could go and if you didn't want to end up in Russian hands you would stay on the road to Vienna and for no reason would get off road meaning that if there were three naked girls on a side road you would not go there. If by train, you got off at St. Joseph at the end of the line. Also, you did not go into the Russian section of the city. We got the feeling they didn't like us.

I forgot to state why we were stationed at this particular area of Austria which was governed by the Russians. When making the agreement for governmenting of Austria, we got the air base even though it was in the Russian section. The reason for this was to give the US big man a place to come and land when he came to Vienna for a meeting of the four powers. So that is the reason I was sent to this beautiful airport.

Now, why specifically was I sent to this Air Base, one hundred miles into the Russian territory from Germany to Austria. The Sargent running the office at this base had put his four years in the service and was going home. The Air Force had a system of numbering the Air Men according to their jobs in the service. My number was 28162 when I got out of the school. This number was the same for every Airmen on every base in the world. As you learned and time went by, the number would be raised to 28263 and at this time that was my number which allowed me to run an office on a base. Why Austria, at this time that person was going home, and this person had the right number, "High O Silver."

So, I shut my mouth, packed my goodies and headed for the train. The special Airmen with special jobs would go by plane so they would not fall into Russian hands, but the Airmen like me would go by train. This train would make many stops, so it took most of the day to get to Vienna. Got there, was picked up, and we went about 30 miles to the base. As we pulled up, I was impressed by a beautiful building. The complete building was stone and beautifully built. In the states the service buildings are a bunch of wood with a roof and the insides are not any better – fancy outhouses. Well, as I stood there looking at it, the thought was- the job may be lousy, but the living quarters would be first class. Spent the rest of the day setting up a very spacious room that I had alone and went to bed for a good sleep.

Next day I was introduced to the men and to my chair and desk in the office. Everything seemed OK but time will tell as this is not what I signed up for. The head man of the squadron was a pilot on a bomber during WWII who decided to make the Air Force a thirty-year living. Government jobs have a very good payoff at the end of thirty years. Well, he may have been a very good pilot but as a leader of men he was inadequate. Me, being the head person of the office, ran the day by day business and added the aiding of the captain when necessary which was most of the time running of an office. I had to tell him what paperwork had to be done and when. This was the way all office operations were conducted. The problem with that way was that I was held accountable for most everything that he had to do and whew, then he would go on a rampage if something was wrong. My ability to do his job was resented by him so most days in the office were not very pleasant. The only day when he was pleasant during the month, was fly day. One day of each month, he would take the Charlie 47 (this is what we called it) to get something for our Squadron. This usually was just a box of whatever. In addition to a happy day flying, he was paid $100 to stay "up" on flying. But unfortunately, it was only one day a month.

When the workday was over, it was rather a nice place to be. We had a bar room with 15 cent German beer, free peanuts, and so forth. The old boys told the new boys, of which I was one, that they would take us to Vienna and show us some of the good bars and good girls. I could not go with them because we were not allowed to go to Vienna in our Air Force clothes, some goofy idea between the powers. So, I had to write a letter home for some of my everyday clothes and that took the best part of two weeks, but it did come. Going to Vienna was very convenient as the train was about twenty feet from our front gate- nice what. The train was not the fastest because it stopped at every town between our town and Vienna, but it only took about a good half hour. It stopped at the Joseph station in the big city of Vienna.

The station is only about 10 minutes from the center of town so, we walk. Vienna is a very nice city of about 160,000 people plus the surrounding city sections. Plenty of great restaurants and food (Viener snitzel) a great many German type bar halls with German type beer – (smooth as a baby's cheeks) around 8% alcohol. What more could a young boy want – girls. Like any big city, there were many young girls, and most of them liked Americans (remember, about five years ago we freed them from Hitler).

Most of the Airmen at our base spent the weekends in Vienna doing what boys do. One of those weekends included going to their "jazz houses" listening to American jazz and drinking the good beer. At this particular bar there was music, the type I liked the best, and played as well as the bands in New Orleans. Somehow, we got to talking with one of the Austrian college students and the main subject was old jazz. One of the boys said, "We have three of this type of music in Vienna, if you wish I can call you when one is in town." This was the best thing I had heard since I got here. They were very good, this was like going to New Orleans, and not nearly as far.

About two months later I got a call that a famous pianist that was an interpreter of Beethoven, but also liked American jazz was playing at a certain bar. I was going (as I often do) with Scotty, a 5-foot 4-inch wrestler at the University of Minnesota, and good. He must have been, because he had a full ride scholarship for four years in school. Scotty learned the German language in six months in Austria and knew it well. Scotty had one problem- he couldn't manage money, so he came to me. Sometimes during the last third of the month he would tell me he needed toothpaste and had just run out of money. So, I would give him money to make it until the end of the month. When he got the month's money, he came first to me and paid up. We paddled the boat in the same direction.

So, I told Scotty about the music in town and he said, "Let's go!" So that evening (weekend) we took the train to town and walked to the bar. We opened the door and looked at each other and said the same thing, "There is no room." That big room was crammed full of people and we were ready to leave when a young man came over and said, "Come with me and I will make a place for you," and he did. There were mostly large round tables in the room, he walked over to one and asked the people to please move over. They did, and he got two more chairs and said, "Enjoy." Scotty sat on my left, and I'm on the left next to two fine looking girls. The pianist did not show up, but they had a good German type band playing German type music, very good.

Scotty was "taken" by the girl setting next to me and started jabbing me on the ribs and telling me to talk to the girl. I let him know that she didn't look like that type of girl that would like American boys in the service. He said, "Nothing ventured, nothing gained," and jabbed me again. Well, to please him and to have something to do (although I have long ago forgotten what I said) small talk probably. But, it wasn't long and we were having a conversation, not heavy but interesting, what service I was in, what state I am from, am I in school, what school did she go to (they have three types of school), where does she live, where does she work and much more of the same type. We had a very nice discussion and it was getting close to quitting time, all of the sudden I got another jab in the ribs and Scotty said, "Get her phone number." I told Scotty that I was sure that she had no interest in continuing the evening for many reasons, one big one, I am an American six thousand miles away. He still didn't "hear" me, so I continued running my reasons for a no and to save my ribs.

So, to stop the game, I asked her for her phone number. She smiled and picked up a match book from the table and wrote her phone number in that and handed it to me. I was flabbergasted, but also a bit happy. But I didn't expect to call, I just wanted Scotty to stop nudging me. So, we said goodbye and headed to the train station and back to the Air Station.

About a week and a half nothing was said, I thought Scotty had forgot, the whole thing was over, but no way. One day at dinner he asked if I had phoned the girl yet? I said, "Scotty knock it off," but he didn't, and he mentioned it almost every day. So, I thought I would make the call and that would be the end of it. Not so, on the phone we made a date at a coffee house for the weekend. We had a nice time catching up our different backgrounds. We also made a date for the next weekend and for many weeks in the future. Scotty said that he took the credit for bringing us together, and I could not argue with that while looking at that smile.

While the time was passing, we spent more of it together and I do think that if that happens, it is love. Most of life revolves around that person and after some time you come to the position, thoughts, ideas, feelings, and more that you wish to spend the rest of your life with her if she has the same feelings. So, it is time to pop the question, I get on my knee, do the popping, and get that wonderful smile from my future wife.

That was just a good start as the next move would be to ask her father for her hand. Now this is more difficult for me than the average male because we do not speak the same language, and later in our happiness I found out that dad was not happy losing his favorite child to another country. But we had our talk with Gertrude being the interpreter between us. But dad wasn't smiling. It wasn't that he didn't like me, but he spoke no English and stated that he had not lost anything in this country, as stated to his daughter. He was going to lose much but I was going to gain very much, love is beyond its understanding. Gertrude, much later, told me that her father had my family monitored before he would allow the marriage, smart.

We set a date in October, but that would conflict with dad being out of the country for a painting he had started sometime before. So, we moved it up a month. Gertrude found us an apartment and that same day we went to one of the pastors that has to check Gertrude to get her into the US. We went into the building and was ushered into a room. After about 10 minutes, a man dressed like a Catholic father walked in and gave us his name, OK why are we here? It was to explain to us that it was to check Gertrude's moral state and to see if she was "good" enough to come to the states. We talked for awhile and the subject of religion came up and we stated that we were Christians. But he asked the question of what type or school of Christianity we were, and we stated that Gertrude was a Catholic and I a Protestant. His face changed, he closed his papers, looked at us for a few minutes and said, "I can't sign these papers if she is going to follow you and become a Protestant and he was without saying a thing more. We still needed to have the papers signed so Gertrude could go home with me. We looked around and found a person who explained the deal. We could have the papers done by the Lutheran's pastor, but he was on vacation for the next three weeks.

That was OK to get the papers, but that would cause a big problem. The president said the war was over and everyone in the service could come home. The problem was that I had to have all papers, including Gertrude's done a week from that time, which was one week before the pastor would be at work. That took me from going home three months before my four years' time was up – January 5. Oh well, that's life, you know the saying of that. There was one nice thing of staying there three months, we could be staying for Christmas and New Year's with Gertrude's family. But considering my feeling about the military, I don't think I would have chosen that operation. So, on January 5th we spent a half of the day kissing, hugging, crying, and saying that we would see each other soon, and we left by rail for Bremer Haven.

Our boat (I have forgotten the name) was nothing special on the outside or on the inside. The military got the bottom (not the officers) and the non-officers and I, mean the bottom. We were assigned bunks two high and very small. The officers and the women were in separate rooms – many more military (male) than female on the bottom.

All was going well for three days until the night that things took a turn for the worse. We ran into the remains of a hurricane and by the next day the boat was plowing through big waves with the front of the boat- I mean much of the big boat front was buried in the wave. When this would happen, the stern would lift so the propeller would speed up (it was out of the water) and make a lot of noise. This would make an unbelievable set of major problems. First it caused about 98% of the passengers to puke in many places, some not made for that. Second, because of the puking, the bathrooms had about 2-3 inches of the stuff, now that was a new type of "happiness." Third, there was a fretful type of female, that because of the noise of the propellers, went about telling anyone who would listen, the boat had a cracked bottom because of the big waves. Now that little message had many of the type who believe anything they hear, but after a day, cooler heads got it quieted down- as one man said, "Madam if that was true we would all be fishing on the bottom of the ocean." Next because of the condition of the boat, 98% of the passengers were not eating- nothing. On the second day I went to breakfast and in a room big enough for 100 people, there were exactly three passengers at the tables, and I was one of them. The food was in garbage cans and that day it was wasted. After a day and night of this, crackers and water were handed out to a lot of suffering to settle the gut down. My wife had no food for three days and she had to tie her jeans with a rope, so as to hold them up.

As with all things, the bad things that we can't control do pass. The fifth day we were able to see New York before sundown, we were docking. Because it was dark, and there were so many personnel, we stayed on ship until the next morning which took a big part of the next day. We had to wait for my duffel bag and all of the rest of Gertrude's stuff. Gertrude being in the top of the ship, got off much before me so she walked in the building until my part of the hull was called- and it was the bottom of the hull but it didn't bother me any time of the trip, but it was uncomfortable, noisy, cold and smelly.

The next morning, we headed for Boston and Gertrude's Aunt (sister to her mother) and Uncle. They were in the US because of Hitler. Her uncle was half Jewish and so, they left as soon as Hitler took Austria over. We had a nice five day stay- a beautiful meal at a famous restaurant, a drive around the city, an evening watching the Boston Hockey Team (Uncle was a captain of the Austrian Hockey Team in the 1938 Olympic games), so he knew many of the big boys in the hockey game, so we just walked in waving our hands and sat in the best seats, Boston won. After the game we had a very nice evening dinner with their friends.

The next morning, we had breakfast and got on the train to Detroit. My dad and my uncle met us the train station and we headed for Muskegon. When we got there the whole family was waiting—that was a big one for a number of reasons. The rest is history.

My brother, dad, and me after the war.

# Epilogue

As I stated at the beginning of my story, this effort was created for my grandson, and my great grandson when he can read and understand. All the times that I got stopped, turned, or told to say nothing, or else there would be a very unhappy consequence. During my not being able to sleep after she died, I began to classify my time in the service. As the time went by, I began to recognize the times that I was not allowed to do what I wished. I began to better understand the "work" of the Holy Spirit in bringing me to the place where my future wife would be. God knew my personality better than I. I was a very blessed man and when I pray, I thank God for the direction that gave me the finest woman in the world.

After talking and being with the kids I explained to the kids, Jacob and Felicity, how the Holy Spirit has put you together, and "Great Grandfather" hopes that it is for the long walk.

Me and my wife

My son.

My wife and her sister.

# About the Author

---

The author grew up in Muskegon, Michigan. He was drafted into the service. Through reassignments he met the love of his life at a Jazz concert in Vienna. He married, raised a son and hunting beagles, and taught school in Michigan.

Printed in the United States
by Baker & Taylor Publisher Services